The Mountain Troubadour
2025
Vol. 71

Montpelier, VT

The Mountain Troubadour: Issue 71 ©2025 The Poetry Society of Vermont

Editor
Erika Nichols-Frazer

Editorial Board
Eileen Brunetto, Caitlin Gildrien, Judith Janoo, George Longenecker, Elizabeth R. McCarthy, Carol Milkuhn

Intern
Harmony Belle Devoe

All poems published in *The Mountain Troubadour* are written by members of the Poetry Society of Vermont. *The Mountain Troubadour* acquires first rights only. All other rights are the author's.

Release Date: June 30, 2025
All Rights Reserved. Printed in the USA.

ISSN: 0027-2604
ISBN: 978-1-57869-203-3

Published by Rootstock Publishing
an imprint of Ziggy Media LLC
Montpelier, VT 05602
info@rootstockpublishing.com, www.rootstockpublishing.com

Book Formatting by Eddie Vincent, ENC Graphic Services.
Cover Art by Ashley Anne Strobridge, "New Moon, New Hope," Airbrush on Watercolor Board, ©2024. Used by permission.

No AI training; no part of this book may be reproduced or transmitted in any form or by any means, electronic or mechanical, including photocopying, recording, or by an information storage and retrieval system (except by a journalist or reviewer who may quote brief passages in an academic or editorial review) without permission in writing.

For reprint permissions, or to schedule a poetry reading, contact The Poetry Society of Vermont at info@poetrysocietyofvermont.org.

*Weeks of rain have made rivers
of our trails. Mud fills the meadow,
slurps at my sneakers, and soaks
my socks when I head out to harvest
raspberries and black currants.*

—Matthew Dickerson, "After the Deluge"

2025 TROUBADOUR AWARD WINNERS
For poems published in the previous issue.

Corinne Eastman Davis Memorial Award
Judge James Morehead
"Two Crows Sit," Matthew Dickerson, Winner
"Sonnet for Two," Nancy Gordon, Honorable Mention

Arthur Wallace Peach Memorial Award
Judge Sean Prentiss
"That Wolf Moon," D. Slayton Avery, Winner
"Saint David's Day," CD Williams, Honorable Mention

CONTENTS

Editor's Note 1

Awards & Summer Contests

Carol and Arnold Abelson Award
Three Thousand Four Hundred Forty-Six Documented Lynchings of Black Americans from 1882 to 1968 (a Golden Shovel),
  Cindy Ellen Hill 3
Honesty, Scudder Parker 4

Mary Margaret Audette Memorial Award
At the Atm, daithí 5
Tango, George Longenecker 6
Thinking About Thinking, Kristine Korman 7

J. Richard Barry Memorial Award
Joseph & Roy, daithí 8
Barn Swallows, Scudder Parker 9

Marion Gleason Memorial Award
Tromping Through Woods, Judith Janoo 10
Surely You Joust, David Mook 11

Goldstein Memorial Award
Cotton, Cindy Ellen Hill 12
A Documentary, CurtB Johnson 14

Laura J. Spooner Memorial Award
When I Wore Bark, Matthew Dickerson 16
Knowledge Worth Having, Nancy Gordon 18
Wisteria, David Mook 19

Chris White Memorial Award
Water, Water, Judith Janoo 20
Homesick on the North Esk, Ivy Schweitzer 21

Members' Choice Spring
Vermont, Vernal Equinox, Jennifer Brown 22

The Kitchen Maid, Carol Milkuhn 23
Horizons West, David Kent Young 24
Demons, Cindy Ellen Hill 25
I Wish, Whit Humphreys 26
Night Drive, Alice Wolf Gilborn 28
The Avocado Tree, Ann B. Day 29
To the Pine Tree Looming over the Gihon River,
   Erika Nichols-Frazer 30
I Prick My Tulips, Maggie Eaton 31
Our Words, Corinne Davis 32

Members' Choice Fall
The Abalone Shell, Kathryn Bonnez 33
The Sheep Barn, Elizabeth McCarthy 34
Still Life with Rain, You, & Everything That Is, JT Butler 35
Glimpses of Home, Kate Viens 36
Come with Me, Scudder Parker 37
In June I Listen to *White Winter Hymnal* on the Way To White River
   Junction, Robin Dellabough 38
Chicago Sonnet III: Running South, Cindy Ellen Hill 39
Failing Limbs, Matthew Dickerson 40
The Garden, Rebecca Willis 41
Immersed, David Kent Young 42
To the Weavers of the Unicorn in Captivity, Carol Milkuhn 43

Previously Published
Harvest, Jess Woolford 44
Cowboy Regrets, Buffy Aakaash 45
Voice of the Deep Expanse, Judith Janoo 46
At the Fair, D. Slayton Avery 48
Always About Words, Tom Schmidt 49
Father, Susan Sanders 50

Selected Works
After the Deluge, Matthew Dickerson 51
Ceramics, Anna N. Jennings 52
Ode to an Empty Fridge, Walker Cammack 53

His Grief, Joy 54
carapace, Joy 56
Mixed Girl, Harmony Belle Devoe 57
Aerial Silks, Gordon Korstange 59
Fish Out of Water, Elizabeth McCarthy 61
Once Removed, Kate Viens 62
Gloria, Tamsen Turner 64
Gethsemane, Ina Anderson 65
Here, Kitty, Kitty, Ina Anderson 66
What Spills Over, Whit Humphreys 67
Self Portrait as Mote, Karen Morris 68
Sand and Stars, George Longenecker 69
As We Do, Jennie Pollard 70
After the Storm, Susan Sanders 71
The Lost, Jared Avelis 72
Commuting, Trish Dougherty 73
Sea-Change, Jess Woolford 75
I Write a Letter to Myself, an Old Poet, Robin Dellabough 76
Ornithophobia, Robin Dellabough 77
Summers, Patrick Bradshaw 78
Shooting Star 79
Love: Oil on Canvas, Abstract in Primary Colors, Sharon Darrow .. 80
Mortal Coil, CD Williams 81
Tension, Patrick Bradshaw 83
North Country Winter, Patrick Bradshaw 84
Astral Projection, Ann Barrett 85
Heart Cloud, Ann B. Day 86
Cycling the Kingsland Bay Loop, Elaine Pentaleri 87
Estelle, Elaine Pentaleri 88
What Took You So Long?, Julia H. Fonte 89

Contributors' Notes 92
Friends of PSOV 99
About the Poetry Society of Vermont 99
The PSOV Executive Council 101

EDITOR'S NOTE

Dear Reader,

Thank you for being here, for showing up to the page. Sometimes, that is all we can do; show up, be present. You are here. I believe, as I imagine you might, in the power of poetry, of art, to heal, to help us make sense of things. There is much to say about the troubling state of our state—our world—yet, in these pages, I hope you can find solace, joy, heartbreak, grief—all that makes us human. Here, you will find suffering but also hope; coming to terms with aging and mortality and loss, but also the small joys of life, of nature, of enduring love. Take a moment to sit in wonder with these words. As Buffy Aakaash writes in "Cowboy Regrets," "Expect nothing./ Revel in everything."

The Poetry Society of Vermont (PSOV) is a community of Vermonters, those with connections to Vermont, and those who simply love poetry. And that is what I want to focus on—*community, connection.*

The poems herein represent generations of poets and different perspectives in conversation with each other. The ages of the poets represented in these pages range from sixteen to ninety-five! I especially want to note Ann B. Day, PSOV's longest member, former editor, and beloved poet who has filled pretty much every role PSOV has had over the years. Ann has had more than one hundred and sixty poems published in *The Mountain Troubadour* over the years and I am pleased that her poem "The Avocado Tree" was voted in the top ten in our Fall Contest by PSOV members for this issue. She also has her poem "Heart Cloud" in the Selected Works section. While our 2023 issue was dedicated to Ann, I would like to again acknowledge her many contributions to the PSOV and the poetry community in general. *Thank you, thank you, thank you,* Ann.

In addition to long-time members like Ann, this issue also features the work of one of our *youngest*—if not our youngest—members, Harmony Belle Devoe, the inaugural Youth Poet Laureate of Vermont. Harmony was our intern for this issue and her astute observations and ideas were instrumental to its development. I am grateful for her perspective and her poem, "Mixed Girl."

I am honored by all who share their words and trust us with their work. This is how we build community and bridge gaps. In the words of daithí in "Joseph & Roy," "But most of all,/what it means to huddle and confer,/against the wintry slopes of time." Things may seem bleak, but we can come together over a love of poetry.

I am grateful to the PSOV's Executive Council and Editorial Board for supporting this publication, which has been in print since 1956, and for their tireless work putting it together. Thank you to all our contest judges and workshop facilitators. I am also grateful to the poets represented here, to all who submitted to this issue, and of course to you, our readers. Thank you for being part of this community.

      Yours in poetry,

            Erika Nichols-Frazer
                Editor

P.S. For the second year, we will publish our shortlist on our website, www.poetrysocietyofvermont.org. Be sure to check out those wonderful poems!

AWARDS & SUMMER CONTESTS

CAROL AND ARNOLD ABELSON AWARD
Judge Karin Gottshall

Three thousand four hundred forty-six documented lynchings of Black Americans from 1882 to 1968 (a golden shovel)

> *hard times require furious dancing*
> —Alice Walker

I hold my pain in my body. It is hard.
I disappear behind stars, beyond times.
Make signs of submission that old gods require.
Mob afire, a war ship called the Furious.
When the rope drops, it looks like you are dancing.

Over the oak tree, the Milky Way is dancing.
Gray smoke thrashes limbs in a furious
wind. Spurious prayer is all old gods require
from the kindling on the pyre of these times.
I hold my grief in my bones. It is hard.

Cindy Ellen Hill, First Place

Honesty
(For my brother)

We *had words* two years ago.
Already the specifics are eluding me
but not the fury in your voice
echoing our father.
Perhaps my question
was too harsh
and then my silence
felt like insolence
indifference to a pain
you thought I'd never recognize.
Now it seems no conversation
can suffice to sort it out.

It was the spoken rule
when growing up
we were a good and happy family.
Sometimes we were.
But the rudeness of honesty was
shocking as a pig escaped
a rampage in the making
all forces marshaled
for its capture
till squealing   as pigs do
without restraint   it was returned
terrified   subdued
to the safety of an even stouter pen.

We both know
don't we
how details slip away
injury solidifies into conclusion
and the conclusion
is a shrinking
that can start to feel
like home.

Scudder Parker, Honorable Mention

MARY MARGARET AUDETTE MEMORIAL AWARD
Judge Dianalee Velie

At the ATM

I wanted to get up early.
I wanted to drive in my car.
I wanted to visit my daughter,
But the ATM has eaten my card.

I wanted to go to her classes.
I wanted to travel REAL far.
I wanted to purchase sunglasses,
But the ATM has eaten my card.

So, I'm sitting here quite apoplectic.
My one-week's vacation's been marred.
I'm fiscally, physically ruined,
'Cause the ATM has eaten my card

daithí, First Place

Tango

Cinderella plots to overthrow the prince,
changes her coach back into a pumpkin,
thinks about charwomen's class consciousness—
she's secretly seeing an organizer
from the glass slipper makers' union.

At the ball she wears slippers of fox fur
and felt, made by her lover just for her;
she waltzes with the prince,
who's still clueless—
then her lover cuts in.

Everyone gasps as Cinderella
and her lover swing into a tango
and swirl around the ballroom
right past the prince
as they plan their revolution together.

George Longenecker, Honorable Mention (Tie)

Thinking About Thinking

I wonder why?
why I think about it
I think about it constantly

It is not a real value
it gets me nowhere
it shows me nothing
yet I think about it
I'm thinking about it now

I think about my thinking
about my thinking
wondering if my thinking
is making me think about it

I think I am thinking
too much about thinking.

Kristine Korman, Honorable Mention (Tie)

J. RICHARD BARRY MEMORIAL AWARD
Judge April Ossmann

Joseph & Roy

Windswept Lake Eden:
A daguerreotype,
their figures outlined
in black against snow-blinding whiteness
and glassy etched ice.
Hunched over, leaning toward
the ever-gaping augered hole,
they sit upon their cooler,
a perfect pair.
Notice how Joseph,
freckle-faced and wide-eyed,
takes in Roy's instructions--
how to hold the jig;
how to bob the line;
how to attach minnows,
or disattach perch eyes, for bait,
with the flick of a thumb.

Then, when to twitch the jig
or how to tend to the tip-up
when its flag flips high,
surrendering its orange nylon wing
to the hungry eyes of the fishermen,
like a raven plummeting and tumbling
against a piercing wind.

But most of all,
what it means to huddle and confer,
against the wintry slopes of time.

daithí, First Place

Barn Swallows
(For my grandson Cashel)

Here millennia before the barns they're named for
they promptly claimed the beams and rafters
and perpetual refuge of sun-stippled dusk   motes
drifting weightless   light-shafts between boards.

Fields torn from forests had exploded
into daisies   summer grasses   black-eyed susans
asters   sprawling purple vetch   and teeming webs
of creatures there for lightning capture on the wing.

They dove through openings—one a fist-sized
outline of a barn cut out for them—to nests
pasted on hand-hewn wood. Each summer haymows
filled with fragrant bales   inching

toward raucous open mouths   urgent   wider
than the tiny heads they hinged.   And we were urgent
too   piling summer in. We could not tell who
welcomed whom. They never bragged about

their longer residence. My grandson has a friend
whose grandfather lives in the Valley who still hays
some fields   fills an old barn. We visit. Swallows chatter
from the rafters. I embarrass him in yet another way—

trying to name the ordinary joy of days we shared
dwelling in each other's company.

Scudder Parker, Honorable Mention

MARION GLEASON MEMORIAL AWARD
Judge Geof Hewitt

Tromping Through Woods

> *Practicing Peace in Times of War*
> —Pema Chodron

Awakened hearts of snow anemones forge upward,
parting the sea of needles and wet matted leaves
by the brook, hoarse from roaring of courage needed
to pierce winter's freeze, reveal butter centers,
ivory cheeks untainted, unsquashed, pristine.
Anemone, you're lightning, early ease, unstirred
stroke of amazement painted among pines,
abiding stem-still until you open, gentle-tongued
as vireo answering its own questioning song,
calling out, how fast I callous in the cold
of unkind words, acts, lash back, add to shared suffering.
Anemone's sure sepals, tender power,
rhizomes multiplying in ground that appeases
what's hardened against another, in me.

Judith Janoo, First Place

Surely You Joust,

but tell me anyway, how so many
"knights in shining armor" become
leftovers wrapped in wrinkled tin foil,
lying for days in the dungeon darkness

behind the closed refrigerator door.
Yes, the light does go out. And yes
Margaret, there is a Santa Claus.
But you'll not find him dressed

in full armor. More likely a red suit,
and maybe a little flushed in the face,
embarrassed by that twinkle in his eye,
or his lance. And even though lacking

in chivalry, he'll still be up for some
jousting. So you'd do well to feed him
your own home-baked cookies. Toss
all of your leftover nights to the dogs.

David Mook, Honorable Mention

GOLDSTEIN MEMORIAL AWARD
Judge Bianca Stone, Vermont Poet Laureate

Cotton

The thread that makes the lace
is just
an ordinary thread,
spun by machine

white cotton
grown in Kazakhstan
its roots
long gone to feed the pigs

those snorting swine
with bristly hairs
devouring
white dangling lines
hanging from prickly stems
and drooping leaves

a harvester that dines on
diesel fuel
removes the boll
then combs and smooths
removes the small black seeds

it's hot
a breeze soft-gently blows
through small-lovely patterned holes
across the dappled shade
of summer skin

strong hands still hold the knives
that slit the throats

of all those pigs

smoke swirls soft-relentlessly
across a searing sky

> Cindy Ellen Hill, First Place

A Documentary

Kings are assassinated and sent here.
Outside the monastery, a procession-
sick monks on litters, and then
the corpse lowered clumsily
like it was a cat killed by accident.
Incense and bells.

From Antarctica to the Battle of the Somme, 1916,
women and children dance around a burning bier.
Men weave nets, eat larva, go cliff fishing.

For a moment in Hong Kong and New York
everyone pauses at their keyboards.
In a tenement he and his wife complain about rats in the basement.
Or maybe it was in a penthouse, and they both agreed,
"You just can't find good help anymore."

The runner in repose.
The runner running.

Caribou cross the river in their annual migration,
as they dig out the miners, three out of 35 half-alive.
In Paris homeless sleep in nooks and parks along the Seine
as people walk to work, shops open.
In Nunavut an Inuit crawls into bed with her husband,
improbably dreaming camelias floating in ice flows.

The soldier shooting.
The soldier is shot.

"It seems like the whole city has
come out on the streets today to greet the President.

Wait, the convertible, it's speeding up...
Something is wrong here.
Something is terribly wrong."

                          CurtB Johnson, Honorable Mention

LAURA J. SPOONER MEMORIAL AWARD
Judge James Crews

When I Wore Bark

When I wore bark,
planted my toes deep
in the earth,
you stood beside me
Just as firmly rooted.

When a gentle breeze
brushed your branches
against mine, I felt
your touch, as tender
as the air, though our bark
has grown rougher.

The cardinal that
sat on your upper branch –
the one broken off
by last winter's ice –
visited me too, though
I could see no red.

When I traded colors
for the *feel* of light,
sound for the feel
of footsteps on earth,
blood for sap,
we drank the same rain.

When wind blew fierce
stripped loose leaves
you stood naked beside me.

And when we topple,
together or separately,
we will become the same earth.

                        Matthew Dickerson, First Place

Knowledge Worth Having

My husband, a physics professor,
did not know for quite a while
how to change a toilet paper roll
where the paper towels are
that we have gadgets that open jars
though I had used them in his sight,
and professed not to know
where the grocery store is,
when we ran out of milk.

But he has always known
how to end an email with "Lubya."
And in the darkness,
after we've said goodnight
and turned out the light,
how to reach out with his hand
and hold mine for a moment.

                                    Nancy Gordon, Honorable Mention (Tie)

Wisteria

This woody vine clings
to the enormous trunk
of an anonymous tree,
circling the column,
plaiting love knots,
ascending, cresting
high above
in sunlit waves
of pinnate leaves.
White racemes
of fragrant flowers
cascade downward
toward a pool
of shade
below.

We draw closer
in the cool grass
beneath the wisteria,
inhale a potent perfume,
yet I smell only you
and ache
to encircle you fully
within my arms,
and make love
knots of our own,
then and there
in the green grass
in the light of day,
right or wrong.

David Mook, Honorable Mention (Tie)

CHRIS WHITE MEMORIAL AWARD
Judge Nancy Richardson

Water, Water

Everywhere hope beats
From the heart of a cloud,
Sprinkles, showers, rains
Into rivulets, puddles, ponds
Slick with lily pads, skippers, frogs,
Heron lifting from spring-fed currents
Shaping and dislodging stones.

Headlong the blue vein of hope
Carried on the melting face
Of a glacier calving into the sea,
On arctic fox, caribou-moss,
Willow creeping, buoying
White gifts light on its fingertips
Conducting hope's symphony,

Quenching parched land,
Drenching and distilling life,
As seized aquifers and rising
Waves shatter into mist we drink
Like each other's tears,
Like vapor too much
For the air to hold.

Judith Janoo, First Place

Homesick on the North Esk

We have come to see salmon leap
in water dark as stout
churned to deafening froth.

First, they fly up the center
but beaten back, search for slower
eddies where currents sculpt curved

niches in the rock. Finally finding
the steps hewn from the stony gorge,
they stagger upstream

miles from open sea back to natal grounds
to spawn in shallow gravelly beds and die.
They are *diadromous*,

able to live in freshwater and seawater.
Far from home, crouched on the sodden moss,
we feel the wrench of instinct

to feed and fatten in foreign places,
storing the ache that eventually
hauls us home.

                              Ivy Schweitzer, Honorable Mention

MEMBERS' CHOICE SPRING

Vermont, Vernal Equinox

Bright as metal catching light
and as hard to look at, hard
to look away from. My eye
hungry, wants to drink in all
the light, all the blue and dark
feathers of treeline writing
contours of ridge and ravine,
engraving land into air.
At the tallest mountain's top,
gray wisps pass over, spit snow.
Up the mountain and back down
in the car's back seat, my ear's
tubing's confused. This human
body isn't wired for such
precipitous rise and swift
descent. This overview, this
big picture dazzles, dizzies.
Shouldn't the whole arc take years,
not minutes? We park the car
and walk. Tracks cross the river—
a fox leapt easy from bank
to snow-cushioned stone to bank.
The waterfall's grown teeth all
winter, now they're loose and shine.
We make snowballs and bowl them
down softening hillside to see
how far, how big, before they
break on trees or come undone
from within. Knowing full well
we all fall down, we're rooting
hard for each makeshift wheel to
make it a little farther.

Jennifer Brown, First Place

The Kitchen Maid

Undisturbed by Vermeer's nearby presence,
the maid is pouring milk with a singular concentration,
as intent on her task as the artist is on his.
Seeping through a window, light bathes the kitchen,
a quiet radiance that highlights her blue skirt,
reaches the fastenings of her yellow bodice,
the edges of the bread in the basket, her apron,
the brass bucket, even a nail and the tiny rough patches
in the white plasterwork of the wall—

and yet Vermeer focuses on her hands—not on these objects—
builds his composition along two diagonal lines
that meet at the maid's wrist, drawing us into the painting
as she tilts the pitcher, keeping the flow steady,
so that we almost hear the trickle of milk,
almost feel the weight of the earthenware,

four hundred years later.

                                      Carol Milkuhn, Second Place

Horizons West

Tonight, a fair wind fills my sail.
Aurora dances 'cross the bow.
This ship is old – its timbers frail
and may not take another gale,
but I must focus on the now.

I sail the course life grants to me,
though wind and weather try the mast.
So seldom serendipity
provides a course through peaceful sea;
hence, I've survived a stormy past.

As I keep sail, I'll do my best
to steer a course bereft of shoals.
I'll put this old ship to the test
until I reach horizons west
and cross into that sea of souls.
(Quintilla)

David Kent Young, Third Place

Demons

What frightens me the most when I recall
that night is not his attack, but my sheer
delight to crush his throat, to smell his fear,
the sight of his phone smashed against the wall,

the way my feet danced, slipping his roundhouse--
caught with my shoulder cap and not my face,
where, had it landed, might have knocked me dead.

I do not think of him at all. Instead,
I think about that powerful dark place
lurking in the center of each of us—

a home to demons fueled by murderous rage,
stone cold and yearning for the fight. We use
their fury, defensive might -- but set loose
to roam, they may not go back in their cage.

Cindy Ellen Hill, Fourth Place

I Wish

I wish I could put
between the striated layers
of my clean T-shirts in the basket,
waiting for you to fold them,
a treat, a real eye-popping wonder,
which would rock you back
and turn the light around you
into a golden embrace.

And in the draining of
Thursday's dinner dishwater,
I find not only forks and spoons,
but that vast landscape
of interlocking energy and beauty
Whitman saw as human-skinned exuberance,
Blake saw in his cosmic grain of sand,
and I see as the universe in the green pea
stuck in the drain.

The mosquito who survived
all the doors, halls and swatting hands
to navigate this deep into our labyrinth,
and to indecisively, momentarily
land on the word *wonder*, above,
shall live! The simple code
which runs its seeking
also runs mine.

The wok stored on the fridge top
made audible the death spiral
of a fly inside as round and round
it bashed against the metal.
You wondered what critter was afoot,
so I checked in the morning

and found rudiments
of the music of the spheres
in that emptiness.

                    Whit Humphreys, Fifth Place

Night Drive

The road's turned into a snake
yellow stripe down its back; headlights
blaze toward me, houses I recall by
day now black silhouettes unknown.
Nameless roads lead nowhere.
I've lost my bearings in the dark.

I've lost my landmarks while I ride
this route, letting it carry me, decide
for me, not out of pleasure but fear—
of cars crossing the center line
deer bounding from woods I cannot
see, lay of the land altered.

My bearings gone, I wonder if my
mind is next, untethered from familiar
signs of daylight, towns that take a block,
a creek, its bridge, hills that rise.
My street, my house. I'm driving
in a dream, my vision changes

in the dark, I ride a snake with yellow
stripe. Without calamity. Slowly I grow
aware of night, how it wraps me, eases
me, transforms mountains into hills.
I've lost my bearings in the dark
I've found another landscape.

Alice Wolf Gilborn, Sixth Place

The Avocado Tree

My six-foot avocado tree
is old; it sits in a fat clay pot
on the floor in my living room.
It sprouted from the pit
of a fresh, ripe avocado
I planted twenty years ago.
A dear friend had plucked it
from her favorite garden tree
when I last visited her
in her South Florida home.

Today it leans its skinny trunk
into the winter window light,
leaves droop and the bark is
scratchy and dry.
The nourishment I give it
seeps into its red clay saucer.
Visitors to my Vermont home
tell me it needs water.
"It's just old," I say.

My Florida friend
dozes in her wheelchair
by the nursing home window.
An IV line runs from a plastic bag
above her slumped head
down to her dry bony wrist.
"Your bag needs refilling,"
an aide says, bustling around her chair.
"I'm too old," she whispers,
her eyes still closed.

Ann B. Day, Seventh Place

To the pine tree looming over the Gihon River

You will fall.
No fighting it now–
inevitable.

It will not be your fault but that
does not ease the splintering,
the crack and crash.

The water bone-shiver cold.

What will remain? What will grow
in your place?

A ghost of you, stump and roots,
your corpse washed away
by icy currents, your place
on the bank forgotten.

And who will bear witness?

Who will remember?

Erika Nichols-Frazer, Eighth Place

I Prick My Tulips

I prick my tulips with a pin
It seems savage
To pierce the gentle succulent flesh
and tear its filament
Green-lanced stems
siphon water
Blooms rise like sunrise
Turbaned queens
statuesque
Lucid color
transparent
Rainbow floods the window sill
Fear and dread dissipate
like spring rain

                                            Maggie Eaton, Ninth Place

Our Words

Pages torn apart,
carelessly strewn about
in the wet muddy streets.

We are blinded by playing
word games and speak
in foreign tongues.

How clever we are to twist
and turn our words into
just what we don't want to say.

The dead weep in their graves
ashamed of the spectacle
that we have become.

Corinne Davis, Tenth Place

MEMBERS' CHOICE FALL

The Abalone Shell

In a souvenir shop on Galveston Island
from a glass shelf beyond my reach
my father carefully delivered it
into my cupped hands
where I cradled the shallow bowl
and felt the hide
of its rough, gray back –
armor once protecting
the soft animal inside

where now swirled peacock colors,
rivers of pearled iridescence –
blue-gray bleeding into ultramarine,
rippling into violet;
ribbons of turquoise
shimmering
like an aurora borealis.

All the way home to Houston
I stared at the shell
and knew as a child knows –
the same alchemy that created
this palette of blues
in the mud-brown waters
of the Gulf

plunged me into all the hues
I could imagine
of still unknown seas
and back into the perfect blue
of my father's eyes.

Kathryn Bonnez, First Place

The Sheep Barn

now empty but for spiders and swallows
        who weave and swoop

through dusty beams of light
        like gauzy dreams — familiar

yet vague

memories that smell of lanolin and hay
        carrying sounds of baas and bleats

to the loft above where sister and I
        sat and watched

lambs in spring search for their mothers
        among the woolen crowd below

until it was time to descend a wooden ladder
        and lead our flock to pasture

out of the old barn
        into the morning sun

                      Elizabeth McCarthy, Second Place

still life with rain, you, & everything that is.

in a dream last night
i remembered the location of an umbrella i had been
searching for

today it rained
so we shared a space
underneath its bent but
assured cover
on the sideline of a game—

one soft drop on an exposed pantleg becomes two
becomes ten becomes us
a part of everything that is—

o for this fold
to be so infolded
o for this softening rain
to be so rain
o for this time of year
to be in time
with you—

i send thanks above the rainfall the heavy clouds
the lightness in your eyes
the dream that allowed for this
generous allowance
of time

& like a magic trick
i send this little joy around your back & back to the beginning
of everything i have dreamed
until now
all the
rainsome & lovesome deluge
of it-

JT Butler, Third Place

Glimpses of Home

"A house has to breathe,"
the old man said.
"They build houses too tight, nowadays."
A philosophy lesson
or a note from the Builder's Guide?

The former, I think. As I watch,
the carpenter grips the dowelled handle of his long oak toolbox and
  in a blink lifts it, mindlessly,
saws, planes, hammers balancing
in thin air

Beneath his thick, hard palm,
every chisel in the pocket he made for it,
every job of the last fifty years
recorded in the cracks, nicks, and paint spatters
of the worn wooden box

We talked of dampness among the rafters
as he fit the louvered panel into the gable
with no time for me to make amends
for hiring an old man to kneel
in the close attic

Specks of dust floated in shafts of sunlight.
"A house has to breathe," he said,
as he plodded down the stairs

                              Kate Viens, Fourth Place

Come with Me

Join me
in the pasture
where placid brown cows
cut paths
across the slope
and trample ripe mud
near the spring
that sprouts
in the knoll's crease.

Listen to the small
explosions of their tasting
long inhalations
of their drinking.

Sit beside me
on the familiar boulder
where moss grows brittle
in the bright eye of the sun
and miniature grey lichen columns
bear red-lipped bowls
across the rusty quartz.

I haven't gone for years.

How could I have known
I was waiting for you
even then?

Scudder Parker, Fifth Place

In June I Listen to *White Winter Hymnal* on the Way to White River Junction

Fleet Foxes sing of red scarves in snow.
Yesterday, the three-year-old declared
he'd seen a fox in aching green dusk.
Purple loosestrife, yellow lily embroider
roadsides, a swell of flight floods this body,
soars in nowness. Last night's dream,
baby from mute to laughing, licks
today. And all my hearts swim
in their own rivers, upstream or down.
I tread in middle clearness, head bursting
out of current again, again, split open
by grace to catch one rainbow trout
arcing between water and air.

Robin Dellabough, Sixth Place

Chicago Sonnet III: Running South

The years have piled on me, an accretion –
the way sand grains accumulate inside
a river's curve, while with the same motion
the outer bank erodes. This is my life,
an ever shifting course whose direction
is preordained. There's nothing to decide
except which name I will call the Ocean
and when my body will merge with the tide.

One time, I saw the Merrimack in flood
meet the incoming spring tide with such might
that ships were torn in two. In Chicago,
they turned the river upside down—its flow
runs south, away from the Great Lakes, like blood
rushing through veins when one puts up a fight.

Cindy Ellen Hill, Seventh Place

Failing Limbs

A grand old maple on the slope below
our house lost one more limb, this one as stout
as a trunk. The tree has suffered from drought
and wind, from woodpecker, disease, and snow.
And from time. It will return to the soil
from which it grew. To fungus, fern, and moss.
Though in its absence I will feel a loss,
I receive the gift of firewood. I oil
and sharpen my chainsaw blade, and pour gas
into the tank. Cutting each log aware
of stiff arms, cranky shoulder. I take care,
hoping the pain in my back will soon pass –
pain of an eternal spirit who must,
before I rise, fall to ashes and dust.

Matthew Dickerson, Eighth Place

The Garden

I ask you to sit in the garden
And you try
But it is raining
Oppressive, unceasing.

And I am confused
Because I'm pointing out the flowers, their colors, their scent.
And the sun through the leaves is dancing so gently
Like we did when we first met.

But you cannot see the beauty.
For we are two people having two picnics
Together and at the same time.
One of us is sitting in the rain.

Rebecca Willis, Ninth Place

Immersed

Oh, to be immersed within the depths
of a captivating poem –
as if to dive upon a coral reef,
weightless as I roam

there, where emotions – each and all –
are seduced, then coaxed and teased,
as if caressed by countless dancing tentacles
of the reef's anemones;

where the colors of its imagery
are all perceived to glint and gleam,
as a vivid splash of rainbow
conjured deep within a dream;

where sensual are its rhythms,
like the rolling waves that play and race
up there above the calmness
of this vibrant, foreign place.

Its resonance flexes, poignant,
as it ascends and then succumbs
like the echoes in these waters –
these clear waters I've become.

As I meld into this ocean,
I feel my senses whisked to froth and foam.
Oh, to be immersed within the depths
of a captivating poem.

David Kent Young, Tenth Place (Tie)

To the Weavers of The Unicorn in Captivity
The Cloisters, New York City

I want naught to do with glorifying hunters,
with tapestries that depict a unicorn impaled--
and so I was delighted by your famous portraiture,
by your vision of a unicorn as alive and well,
a mythical, Christ-like creature, peaceful and pure.

Your unicorn rests within a circular fence,
linked to a thriving Pomegranate—he is not chained,
captured, confined—he is a being in suspense,
choosing to remain in captivity, his noose,
a fragile belt of gold, an artistic pretense.

I marvel at the magic that worked through your fingers,
let you wrap silk in metallic, dye wool with weld,
to create low fences, chains that do not hinder,
as well as cloven hooves, horn, and milk-white fur—
here are threads woven with gentleness,
                              a touch that lingers.

                            Carol Milkuhn, Tenth Place (Tie)

PREVIOUSLY PUBLISHED

harvest

in those days
in the north country
many great clouds formed
over the farm
& served strong portions of snow
    November through March
        even edging up to May

though thin & tenuous the atmosphere
    transformed tiny hailstones
        & shook them
    spangle by spangle   free

    snow
    on snow
    on Jericho
    where Wilson waited with microscope & camera
        gathered in the glacial grains
        feathered them into focus
        & noted Nature's jewel masterpieces

        then   wonder-working aperture & illume
        eternalized each singular snow crystal
            instants before evaporation

        supremely happy in service to his muse
        he set course
        by the icy stars wafted his way
            & discovered miracles in myriad
            on a cloud farm flourishing at the
            edge of the known

Jess Woolford
the museum of americana: a literary journal, Issue 31

Cowboy Regrets

Some people get thrown from their horse
and get right back on.
If I take the time to get to know a horse
gently mounting its back
engaging in giving and receiving
and it throws me to the ground
horse riding may not be my thing.

What would it take to get up after a fall
unlike so many greenhorns before
and take the reins again?
To find love in what I'm doing
and do what I love?
Whatever it is.
To know the wounds
from that unintended dismounting
would heal in their own time.
To desire something
Anything.
To go somewhere
even a distant place.
To get back on and feel the wind
blow the journey over me.
To not know what I will find.
Expect nothing.
Revel in everything.

Buffy Aakaash
The Whisky Blot, Spring 2022

Voice of the Deep Expanse

Know from the way I'm always changing
the danger of complacency.
   Easy to lull you
      with the rhythm of waves
lapping against rocks, piers,
your sure feet.
   I forge marshes,
      polish wood, glass,
cast plastics across sand,
across sculpted dreams—

but you can count on my rising
twice daily, and withdrawing to expose
   the otherwise hidden,
      still a mystery
to those who haven't seen the sea,
brimming with life.
   I join lands,
      even countries at war
with my blue-green expanse,

I froth and foam, colonize shores
with rockweed, air with brine.
   My steel depths
      conceal mountains,
create clouds the wind sends where it will.

Know from the way I'm always changing,
mournful waves play off deep unease,
   each time I leave my mark
      without malice, erase cliff-side castles
you thought would last more lifetimes,

forgetting your shelter won't feed you

as I can, spanning wind-ripped currents
   to save the drowning human family,
      if they will allow me.

Judith Janoo
Just This, Kelsay Books, 2023

At the Fair

Plaid shirted old men
harnessed in suspenders
lean forward, lurch
with the lunge of muscled ponies pulling
stone boats in the raked dirt arena.
They mouth the simple words a pony knows.
Unweighted memories are skidded easily
to the jingling tune of a doubletree.

D. Slayton Avery
Vermont Magazine, 2024

Always About Words

The tattered photo album in my dream
Falls open to page ten where I sneak in
To Mrs. Campbell's dim fourth grade cloakroom
To seek the satin pocket of Pam's coat
Where I insert the tightly folded square
Of lines furtively spelling out my love.
I shudder at my first submission, turn
To go to class, but this is all I see:
A row of cursive letters, white on green,
Push-pinned into the strip of cork above
A blank black chalkboard covering one wall.
I cannot recreate the rest, the rows
Of restless kids in desks, or even Pam—
Nothing remains except that strip of script.

Why does this snapshot, held by synapses
For more than fifty years, refuse my will
To move beyond a closet and a pocket and
A cursive alphabet to look around
At who and what else had to have been there?

A wonder there's so little left of Pam,
Who owned the coat, and by the way, my heart
Throughout that year, and must a little still
Or I could not have kept her all these years—
Or if not her, at least her precious pocket,
That humid satin place I penetrated
In my dim innocence, a nascent lover
Of words, who even then and even now
From that dark cloakroom cannot see beyond
The cursive letters high on the horizon.

Tom Schmidt
Rowing with Either Oar, Solum Literary Press, 2024

Father,

You will never know how
many nights I spent
working my way out
from under your roof.

Inside your shop of radios
you hid behind safety glasses
testing troubled circuits with a frown.
Outside the thirty-foot tower stood
ready to receive the codes I didn't know.

Is it better for men to speak
through invisible fields of energy?
Brief pauses after greeting
and then on to the facts
of your weathered lives.
Tethered by those connections
you remain tied down by
circumstantial gravity.

Upstairs, the static breaks
the silence that holds us captive.
Miles away on another frequency
I build stories in seconds as you
crisscrossed fine intricate wires
aware of how to bridge
the distance between
here and there, which is closer
than the speed of light.

Susan Sanders
California State Poetry Quarterly, 1990

SELECTED WORKS

After the Deluge

Weeding my way from the pea pods
to the wax beans, I catch a whiff
of decay. I remember a deer once hit
on 116 whose stench lingered for days,
and we could not let our dog off leash.

Weeks of rain have made rivers
of our trails. Mud fills the meadow,
slurps at my sneakers, and soaks
my socks when I head out to harvest
raspberries and black currants.

But the cat concerns me most —
the cat I buried in a cardboard box
late last winter, with the help of my son
who dug into the frozen earth. We later
planted flowers in the soft soil.

Looking at the small lake that
has spread around the cosmos,
and smelling that smell, I wonder
if we dug the hole
deep enough.

Matthew Dickerson

Ceramics

> *River banks colored in layers of history—*
> *a child pokes a stick and digs into sediment:*

I try my hand at the potter's wheel and in time
find a center, cone-shaped on spinning bat.
Underneath clay moves, rounds down
with a steady pressure of the palm.

> *the settledness of stories, the traces of truth.*
> *Mud, water; muddy water—*

Grounded, I open up, explore margins.
Hands dip in clear water, return
to elevate sides. Slowly, thumbs touching,
always one until my imprint, my history

> *my mudpies, drying in the sun.*

becomes part of this earthen vessel
turned, trimmed, marked mine.

Anna N. Jennings

Ode to an Empty Fridge

Eighty-six the chicken liver pâté
and the chanterelle compound butter.

No need for scallop crudo
or fine little tweezers placing borage stars.

Hold the rabbit confit,
the elderflower panna cotta and amaro too.

There's a time and a place
for excess and mise en place–

for celebration of all earth's wonders
and our place in helping them sing–

but tonight, let us squeeze
every ounce of joy

from the dried-up half onion
forgotten behind the pickle jar

and the last garden kale
wilting sweetly to November's frost.

Walker Cammack

His Grief

I.

We make lists together.
We walk in circles all day with our lists in the kitchen.
We get distracted by item 3, forget to finish item 1, and spend three hours
   on item 4.
We go back to our lists.
We laugh at the ridges our feet have danced into all the floors.
We cheer when things are completed.
We make lunch and watch T.V., South Park.
I try to eat so that you will worry less.
We have ice cream with chocolate sauce every night on the couch.

II.

Your five decades of loyalty replaced
her first two decades of trauma
You can't finish the sentence where you are
grateful for the three good weeks she had
within the three bad months of cancer
Your chest shakes because she died in pain
instead of dignity
Your throat moves differently,
swollen shut inside while you try to breathe without her,
holding half the words in,
the rest releasing at half volume.

III.

I want to crawl into your heart with a sewing machine, stitch a seam that will hold you, embroider on all of your cells what it feels like to be silently understood by you.

I want to tell you I am only alive because you are my father.
I want you to know you've done a good job.

Joy

carapace

his tongue carves
lacquered oak relics in my spine
wrapped in Venetian lace

we revel in the sound of our vertebrae
clicking in and out of our merging bodies

he smiles and says I am tiny and made of magic
pulls me to his abdomen
where I curve perfectly into loving him

I am honey oozing from underneath an
unexplainable cadence with perfect pitch

he is a new language
spun into a lexicon of ritual

                                                    Joy

Mixed Girl

I know a girl.
Her eyes are chocolate dahlias.
Her voice,
like a hairpin crescendo.

I know
another girl.

I know a caramel girl,
I know a honeysuckle girl,
I know a Hershey's kiss girl,
she blows a kiss to the sky as she enters school.
I know a walnut girl,
I know an 86% cacao girl,
I know myself,
a cinnamon girl edging on vanilla,
trying to get a hang of
her grandma's language,
wincing
as sweet cream girls gawk
at the night sky girls' wide-hipped walk

I'm tryna' understand
how to talk
to snow-white girls
without abandoning my ancestors,
opposing sides;
the colonizers
and the colonized

I know a girl
she's a milk, and dark, and white chocolate swirl

and girl,
you make me stop
on the sidewalk

because your warm hues glow,
your brown adorns you,
your mix, it shows,
radiating,
I feel my heart pulsating,

my eyes already dilating,
because you're just so captivating,

and I feel you.

Girl, I love you.
I am you.

Harmony Belle Devoe

Aerial Silks

Like a seasoned sailor
   she hoists herself
      hand over hand upwards
         toward the dim rafters
  to lie snuggled above us
staring at startled spiders.

How she twists fabric about her,
    trying on a wardrobe high above the floor,
       swaddled in cloth around her hips,
                legs,
                        feet,
                                arms
then in a flurry of sinuous moves
    weightless dancer she becomes
        a pen du lum
    wrapped only around one foot,
                leg extended,
    abandoning herself   to bare space
O she is safe and alone up there
    fair maiden who is both bound
                        and unbound
winding herself into a mummy
    in and out of an aerial grave
when suddenly   in a few frenetic moves
    she unfurls like a sail
            over and over
and descends through our held breath
        tumbling
          body
            jerked
              to a halt
hovering just above our pleading hands
    leaning forward to catch her

                                self-saved
            rocking in a cloth cradle
lazy
        summer
                backyard
                        hammock.

                                Gordon Korstange

Fish Out of Water

there it was, in center of the dirt road
        an eighteen inch rainbow trout

black speckled spots on its olive green back
        silvery-white belly and light pink sides

still clear eyed and shiny, as if it flopped
        the quarter mile from lake to here

where I stood, stopped on my morning jog
        to stare down at this fish out of water

wondering, how did it get here
        should I pick it up and run,

clean it for dinner, feed it to the cat,
        or leave it as if it were meant to be

there in the dirt like the many
        who are cast into a far flung world

breathless, flat on the ground and gutted

                                        Elizabeth McCarthy

Once Removed

Music whispers, harpsichord floating
over the new carpet
and the tastefully painted walls, wainscoting, and downy wing chairs
into my mother's room.

She didn't want to lose
her old life,
so she gave it to me.
Can you blame her?

I buy tasteful slacks and jackets now,
pay my respects to the old Portuguese tailor
in his shop behind the main street
where he will hem my mother's clothes.

He will ask about my brother up in Maine, whose uniforms he fitted
long   ago,
creased hems reflected in the spit shine
of the patrolman's polished shoes.
My mother's pride reflected in the tailor's eyes.

At the nursery, I weave
past pots of perennials whose habits I know so well.
A graveled path leads me to tables groaning
with geraniums. I buy annuals now.

A hot sigh escapes my car.
I push aside the trowel and watering can
to lay down a tray of crimson petals,
the kind that stain fingers and clothes.

I trudge across the uneven grass,
pay my respects at my father's grave.
I kneel and dig and plant and pray. Holy water

flows beneath my mother's name.

She didn't want to lose
her old life,
so she gave it to me.
Can you blame her?

Kate Viens

Gloria

We followed the tractor like a procession.
Two holding hands, me following from a distance,
numb,
from behind the barn where I fled after dragging the body and
losing my grip

She succumbed to her efforts, after all of ours, for two straight days.

It was spring but windy, the cold still freezing our ear tips and fingers,
fingers that had grasped her body and held her and each other and
pulled at dead lambs fruitlessly
fingers we wove into her wool as she shuddered and slowed her
   heartbeat to a stop.

You were holding her head, her shepherd
guide to the end.

As you lifted the manure pile with the tractor, I
noted your skill through puffy eyes.
How you could still manage all the controls, turn the machine to
   deftly create a space
for her body and the lambs'
and cover them to prevent scavenging.

After the others left we took off our clothes and put them in the wash,
stinking of shit and hay
and molasses and fluids,
crammed together into the shower stall, not wanting to be apart even
   for a moment.

Tamsen Turner

GETHSEMANE

He came to her finally,
she knew he would but, oh, the doubts,
the waiting. First the wafting
of chalk and lavender, the scent

of laundered linen. Then he came
from behind the eucalyptus, stepped
out as if he'd just stepped
into its shadow for a day or two.

And she wanted to run to him, to fall
at his pierced feet with her balms, her sponges,
to ease him, to lay him out on the warm rocks
with cushions under his dear head.

Her feet, though, were rooted.
Then her eyes lifted upwards and she saw
the smile she knew, his eyes, beckoning.
Only then did she move,

move with him to the soft leaves
beneath the cliffs. The warmth of

her night heat still lingered in the bed cloths.
Only then did she fall to her knees.

And when the dawn sprang it was golden
and full of the song of birds.

Ina Anderson

HERE, KITTY, KITTY

Is my cat a poet?
Does he stalk his muse beneath the thick undergrowth,
listening in perfect attention for the rustle of her arrival?
Does he greet her with a glad twitch of his tail?
Do his ears prick at the sound of precise verbs,
cunning nouns, tasty turns of phrase?
At a moment unpredicted, does he pounce
with utmost confidence on the draft
of a well-formed sonnet,
or perhaps just a haiku no bigger than a cricket?
Does he toss it cruelly into the air,
tease it, taunt it, hear it squeal,
until he alone decides it is ready to devour
head-first, crunching it between his needle teeth?
Can I be a poet like him?
And, work done, older drafts discarded,
can I contentedly sleep in the sun?

Ina Anderson

What Spills Over

Years ago, I knelt and cupped
in my hands cold alpine brook water
reflecting morning stars.
I gulped a handful, stars and all,
then threw it on my face
where it remains.
I am all supernova now, high on hydrogen
with a circadian rhythm tied to a local star.

And here we are, you and I,
spinning around that infinite point,
a child's handful of light-years from us,
on the Orion spur of the Perseus arm
in this elegant spiral spinning in the dark.

That the universe has learned to speak through us
is marvel enough, more so that we talk
with each other on this rainy September morning.
I see fusion in your eyes, and the way
space bends a little around your singular smile.

And if there is a multiverse, this is the one I want,
where fire, wind, earth, rain and plant and we
burst through the cosmos' mute indifference.

> Whit Humphreys

Self Portrait as Mote
For John Tomlinson

It was for us that Rembrandt unearthed the untidiness of nature—
thumbed his nose at pundits and The Golden Age, unbuckled
his devouring eyes and hitched them to ours. Crumbs from his pencil
fell in lead-soft licks, in charcoal-points smudges and swirls, dust
serenading dust. Fury perhaps, to raise by lowering the bar, bevel by
microscopic bevel, proof in the rag-soft tourniquet wound round his head.
I'd hazard my heart for just one wink from his wrinkly puss.
It's for him I'd blow the dust off the covers of life-style artists who fail
to endeavor— Just because it's round doesn't mean it's a walnut—
their particles dispersed before their primes in search of the perfect idea,
formulaic about causes and conditions they float in jars of formaldehyde.
His raw, burnt, and somber umbra yield to our graceless time. We fondle
failed experiments; dip them in wax, drip neon, laminate electrodes, stare
into fields of titanium bright enough to be titled, *The Old Master's Nose.*

Karen Morris

Sand and Stars

Venus shines in the east,
one by one stars brighten,
sea grinds stones and shells to sand,
as I lie here on the beach
Little Talbot Island,
distant lights from Jacksonville,
and naval base just south,
where Trident submarines
slip under the sea like whales,
carrying enough nuclear missiles,
to obliterate Florida and Georgia.

Perhaps some other creature,
light years away
on a planet orbiting one of those stars,
lies on a beach,
listens to wind,
as waves grind their planet to sand.
One by one more stars brighten,
we couldn't live on Venus,
but on one of those stars
there's a planet with seas,
sentient beings who write poetry,
design machines to reach other stars.
I wonder if we're the only ones
who can vaporize each other
with fusion as hot as a star.
I'd like to think
somewhere a planet has evolved,
where beings don't annihilate each other.
I lie here, listen to waves,
watch ships' lights, distant stars.

George Longenecker

As We Do

A trail of condensation
mixes with morning light, pinks and golds,
now so far away the plane has gone on
as travelers do.

I stand on the deck as the season
turns suddenly cool. River fog fills
in the valley, lifts closer to our hill,
as autumns do.

It is the sharp light
that holds everything tightly,
grasps birds and leaves,
waning moon and me

close against this early morning.
I hear no sound. My cat has
fallen asleep again
as cats do.

Flickers arrow across the grass
their white underbellies giving them away
preparing to fly south
as birds do.

Now the fog closes me into its moist arms.
All is white and nothing is clear.
I will have to make things up
as I do.

Jennie Pollard

After the Storm

Leaves once lush,
sensuous green
faded brittle brown.
Wind left branches
on cursed ground.

Stilled by this mountain
of silence between
us we both direct our
eyes towards the wide
window as if the sky
could answer.

Winter ties bind the
body down as spring snow
falls very slow. You hold
both of my hands, bid me
back to bed where together
we dream of nothing.

Susan Sanders

The Lost

Found
under pass, within broken
box houses, holed tents
tucked snug against
graffitied concrete
ants lost from a colony
ever blinded to the souls
it has burnt up into grey ash
wisps and hard charcoal chunks.

Found
with pocketknives tucked
into well-worn boots
and scabbed hands shaking
clutching bent steel spoons
charred black yet bliss full
as candied bits of plastic
and gutter milk soak
into a mind full of need
as cruel as a park bench
built to cause insomnia.

Found
adrift with the clouds
that cast shifting shadows
over a brow finally unfurrowed
lines of worry worked loose
by a dissolving moment of relief
from the everything below,
until dawn opens an eye
to see a world
that pretends they don't,
awake in a world
that thinks they won't.

Jared Avelis

Commuting

A bee stung the back of my wrist
bravely I got in the car anyway
probed the sore spot driving one-handed
to go to all the places I didn't want to be
with all the people who exhaust me

Thirty years now driving Subarus
the same route, to the same job, only
the colors & passengers have changed
through months of snowstorms, alongside weeks
of foliage, and hectare beyond hectare of green

Back in the turquoise Impreza days
my youngest had tantrums in his car seat
   hot if we took a different road
   pissed if the radio was on
we all carried books to read until he quieted
pulled over with the hazards blink-
ing

I don't turn on the radio anymore, seldom
deviate from the most efficient route
driving to work I weep nonetheless
belted & powerless like my youngest used to be

I try to be a good Buddhist
to purge myself of desire and thereby
shed all the things that might define myself
-if I am not a person who yearns to retire
am I anything at all?

I don't mind driving, navigating banked turns
in silence, I wish to never arrive, to be alone to cry
in my Subaru the radio off, a book in my hands

beneath the purpling night
to turn on the dome light
& read

                                                Trish Dougherty

sea-change

mother an incantation   of breakers
      drew me from your dark ocean
          seal slick
          spuming indignation
      your tears my sacral spring

seven summers on we slung ourselves
          into shock atlantic swells
              bobbed side by side
                  selkies sharing duplicate drift glass eyes

            when ice jammed my veins
      & blue hued my lips
    you swaddled my shivering
held me as I nuzzled your salt neck

later cancer's red tide tore through you
          too quick to catch
              rogue cells blooming berserk
                      sluiced your spirit free

upon your chapped lips
I set sand dollar seal
pressed an ear to your chest
& heard your blood brine booming
      perigean tide towing me beneath

                        Jess Woolford

I Write a Letter to Myself, an Old Poet

Listen to every drop of drizzle, mizzle,
as if it were your first sound.
Give your tired tongue something sharp: ginger, salt.
Sleep your delicate bones, recollect mislaid words.
Remember to deadhead black-eyed susans,
butterfly milkweed. Yourself.
When your back aches, lie down on patchy grass,
ignore cicada killer wasps burrowing beneath.
They won't be what gets you in the end.
Don't think about your end, swim under,
look for *Turritopsis dohrnii*, jellyfish
that absorb their own tentacles to live forever.
Handle blown glass greedily, linen sheets, a shard of shale.
Grasp all this glory. Give it to the Snow Moon.

Robin Dellabough

Ornithophobia

He names me Robin after his brother
but what if really he craves a bird
to keep close in a nest of rope,
roses, painted wood? He brings me
little morsels of attention, only wants
to teach, not listen to my newly hatched
twirps. I try to fly, to find my flock,
but am afraid. I need to make a clutch,
to settle into a cup of moss, leaves. After
I feed my own fledglings and even others—
blackbird, willow warbler, song thrush—
I'll fold my wings back into skin.

Robin Dellabough

Summers

Again the summer sky
Has gone blue gray
Hazy over the distant lake
A deepness, a promise
Of summers to come
Reminding me of summers past
When the weather broke
And flung the waves up and down
While the boats slopped and banged against the docks.
Lines pinging against the rigging,
Chiming as the moored dinghies
Leapt upon the waves
Deep memories –almost gone
And promises of summers
Extending into the future
A vanishing point at both ends
Closer now at sixty-two
To a different kind of vanishing

Patrick Bradshaw

Shooting Star

Catch a shooting star,
Make it tell you the truth
Of the cosmic egg,
The chaos within,
The goddess bringing life
Upon the waters, and
As you breathe the breath
Of a Narwhal into your heart
Play a melody of Silver Bells
And think of a childhood
Kingdom under the sea
Where immortality
Allows you to sleep for
a day and a month and a year
And when you crawl out upon a shingle
Dream of a moth fluttering in moonlight,
And when you wake, you will weep,
To find your wings exchanged
For feet, and the breath of air
Has been stolen from you
And mortality has pirated your heart
And hope has been given to death

Mary Cheyne

Love: Oil on Canvas, Abstract in Primary Colors

Cover the canvas with brilliant yellow for the first
kind of love, maternal, familiar, earliest family
feeling. Add streaks of orange as yearning grows.
Red jagged lightning strikes from Eros' arrows cut
slices across from corner to side, and alongside,

violet echoes trace across a lover's eyes. Unbidden,
storge, *eros*, then deep green fronds of *philia*
awaken, as friends grow strong, while blue-as-sky
agape leans upon the conscience, absolute, clear,
perhaps god-like, of necessity chosen, rarely

unbidden, a revolution of resolution, a steady pulse,
tide not under the skin, but inside the mind.
Heart follows its wisdom, a consciousness
of choice, allows practice to perfect, its wild
blue ocean to arise from the depths, wash

across the canvas, lap up higher, splash
along the right edge to the top right corner,
dive beyond and pour out onto the wall, floor,
this canvas unable to hold a love that allows
no boundaries to the open seas a human can become.

Sharon Darrow

Mortal Coil

> *For in that sleep of death what dreams may come*
> *When we have shuffled off this mortal coil*
>   —Hamlet, 3.1.66-67

Last night I was cleaning up after supper and I was wondering—

Seven years before I was born my father's father died at 57 from tuberculous;
My mother's father, my Pa whose name I carry, at 64 of cancer;
And my dad? My dad at 69 in the driveway, snowblower running on high throttle.

I know sons bury their fathers—I hadn't seen it a pattern of life in good order—
And learned fathers sometimes bury their children—I never understood that curse until I faced it.

Last night I was cleaning up after supper and I was wondering—
What's the purpose—my purpose—living more years than these who've gone before?
Is my work in the world just not yet finished?
Maybe a challenge, a chance to try, to accomplish more—
Or a gift perhaps, a chance to laugh, to cry more.

I'm coming to understand there is neither gift nor challenge nor curse.
I carry sorrow without, as I've been told to feel, gratitude,
I carry sorrow without, as I've been told to seek, closure.
I carry sorrow beyond days of grief.
In that sorrow I carry memories.
And I endure. For now —

Eventually the mortal coil will slip from my shoulders—
The shroud, inevitable — I expect no grace in its dark folds.
Will the dreams that come include a reunion of souls or quiet, empty nothing?

Last night I was cleaning up after supper and I was wondering and
    I looked down in the dishwater and saw my father's hands.
  Surprised
    I looked up and, reflected in the window over the sink, his eyes.

And that is, I suppose, enough.

CD Williams

Tension

Today I bought a post hole digger
Like a normal person would
Asked about posts and ties
And gates and latches
Welded wire in three and four-foot rolls

The people at the farm store
Answered all my questions
Assuming that I too
Belong in the company
Of practical people
Who build chicken coops
And put up garden fences

I used the right words
And smiled in such a way
That they would never know
Who really stood there

Barely holding it together
And wishing he knew how to let it go
——TING——
Recoiling into space
Like an over-stretched wire
Gone with a snip of the pliers

Patrick Bradshaw

North Country Winter

Down the towers of iron sky
Down, down to where I stand
A bitter mile
Of winter's fortress
Flies up before me

If my feet came loose from the frozen ground
I would fall into the empty air
Rising
Turning slowly
Head over heels
Until I was a speck of black against the gray
And then a speck of nothing

Patrick Bradshaw

Astral Projection

I fly overhead for points north
through a clear January night
to consult cosmological beings.
There, my mother is dining with
Carlos Castanada and Don Juan.
She is smiling, her body subtle,
no longer weighted down with all
she lived in life. Carlos and his mentor
are drinking red wine, my mother—
a Diet Coke with ice — her cheeks flushed,
her eyes glowing. They share a secret,
passing it between them like children
in the schoolyard. I am the outsider,
ignored— they are folded into
their amusement of one another.
Tugged back to the earth plane,
I try to shout: Why—When —?
but my words are silenced as
the heaviness descends. I leave
the realm of the wise ones,
to find my questions
lost, no longer salient here,
in the land where influencers prey.

Ann Barrett

Heart Cloud

Sunday morning
as I walked up
to the courtyard in 85-degree heat
I wondered, is this reality?
When I came back to my cottage
the thermometer on the front porch
read 95 degrees:
was that reality?
Inside it was 83.
I turned on the AC
Soon it was 73 and felt cool.
But is that reality? Outside the porch
thermometer had climbed to 97!
Yet just inside
only feet away
I was comfortable.
Should I be? What is reality?
I looked up to the pines
the oaks, the beeches,
the clouds, the sky.
There was the answer:
a cloud heart promising
the true reality
of hope and courage,
deep friendships and
faith in our future.

Ann B. Day

Cycling the Kingsland Bay Loop

One broad sky, one quiet country road,
one bicycle, one woman.
What counts?
A full sun approaches the twelfth hour.
Paint by number, by revolution, by distance.

Four plush clouds settle
comfortably into the wide blue,
hover lightly above a leafy canopy
of distant sugar maples
at the height of their greening season.

Three late summer cornfields
boast their browning silks and heavy stalks,
two hayfields are pinned
by dozens of neat round bales,
five boisterous crows stake claim.

Two horses graze
by one rustic stable
beneath one circling osprey.
Lean onto the gravelly road
that winds down to the bay.

Six sailboats moor
each to its own floating buoy.
Lapping water warbles on smooth shale
skirting the shoreline.

Set the bicycle against a twisted
white cedar rooted on the rockface
just above the bluff,
where a double-crested cormorant
leaves its rock perch to dive for fish.
On this rounding day
count the soft and tallied riches.

Elaine Pentaleri

Estelle

Call me the other child, the less seen,
sliding between the sturm and drang
of this modern world,
the one who says nothing at the breakfast table
reflecting on the patterns in my bowl and spoon
preferring solitary play in the silence of my room,
alone.
With puppets, musings, marionettes,
I wait for the dreams to come.
I learn quickly what comfort there is
in shadows,
watching from quiet corners
the frenzied affairs
of those vying for favor and place.

The night sky opens to me.
The stars whisper this way, this way
along a lighted path.
Time reels, before and after,
in undulating waves.
I see.

I keep my secrets to myself,
notice the splays of light and pattern
on the yellow wall.
Silence moves mountains.

Elaine Pentaleri

What Took You So Long?

When wildflowers filled my days
and gray specks streaked to silver, you
snuck in dressed as subtle curiosity,

drawing me in with verses
unknown, followed by a raven's visit
to ensure my commitment.

You come to me in the inky night,
waking me from days long past, tears
of grief or love, or maybe adventure,

expecting me to fulfill your needs
at once, before my mind erases
or misconstrues your intended symbols.

I hear your whispers in otherwise
still woods. In meadows
I see your message of renewal

in the textured face of a blood root,
hear your summer joy ring from pink-
striped bells of spreading dogbane.

I did not realize your spirited way
of dropping in without calling first
would become a gift of passion,

change my life, command me
to the page. I never saw it coming.
This was not who I was.

And so I muse on your timing,
knowing better than to question it,
amazed you called

at the height of autumn's radiance,
when snowflakes may begin
to crystalize any time now.

But you know I am willing, eager,
running to catch up despite this ache
for time lost, for time left...

Julia H. Fonte

CONTRIBUTORS' NOTES

Originally from New Jersey, **Buffy Aakaash** lived in rural queer communes and big cities across the US before coming home to Vermont with his dog, Bodhi. He has poems in numerous US publications and abroad. His chapbook, *Untangling the Knots*, was published in 2022, and *Breaking* will be published in 2025.

For many years, **Ina Anderson** edited scientific journals, including *Icarus* with astrophysicist Carl Sagan. She went on to teach writing and literature at Vermont State Colleges. Her collection, *Journey into Space*, was nominated for a Pushcart Prize. Kelsay Books published her collection *Sky Furniture* in 2024.

Jared Avelis lives in Shoreham, Vermont with his wife and two sons. He spends his time walking the forests and fields around his home, taking care of his kids, and listening to music.

D. Slayton Avery was raised on pondwater and blackflies in the wilds of Woodbury. She enjoys playing with words, which is sometimes work. But sometimes her work is taken seriously, with her short fiction and poetry appearing in a growing number of online and print journals and anthologies.

Ann Barrett's short story publications include the *Rio Grande Review* and PKA's *Advocate* (defunct). Pursuing an MFA in Creative Writing at New England College, Ann lives in Vermont with her husband and a ragtag pack of rescue dogs.

Kathryn Bonnez is a retired ESL/French instructor, nonfiction author, and poet. She has lived part-time in Vermont since 2015. Through her poetry, she continues to chronicle her steadfast connection to the quiet mysteries and revelations of her chosen home begun in her memoir of place, *A Lone Star in the Green Mountains*.

Patrick Bradshaw is a retired electrical engineer who has been a secret poet for most of his life. This is his first published work.

Jennifer Brown (she/her) lives in Montpelier, Vermont, teaches at CCV, writes poetry, nonfiction, and a Substack, *Some Day All This Can Be Yours*. Her work has appeared in *Copper Nickel*, *Cimarron Review*, and *Cincinnati Review*. Her poetry collection, *Natural Violence*, was published in 2022 by Brick Road Poetry Press.

JT Butler is a poet, librarian, music lover, & family man currently living in Duxbury, Vermont. He thinks of poetry as a beautiful little world available to everybody, & is overjoyed to play a part in adding bits & pieces to that world along the way.

Walker Cammack spends his days living in a beautiful little valley in Danby, Vermont. He's a trained forester and currently works as the Program Director at a land-based non-profit called the Smokey House Center. Nothing fills him up more than helping kids connect to land and walking the woods with his dog, Nettle.

When **Mary Cheyne** retired, she started writing poetry. She loves writing about nature and likes to incorporate mythology with that. She is often frustrated, really doesn't know what she's doing, but it's fun and she enjoys the challenge.

daithí (he/him) lives with his wife in Montpelier on the unceded land of the Abenaki people. He has published poems in *Tendril*, *Refocus*, and in recent anthologies of PoemCity. His ancestral home rests primarily on what is now called Ireland.

Sharon Darrow, author of novels and picture books for children and young adults and whose poems, short stories, interviews, and personal essays for adults have appeared in literary journals and anthologies, was a member of the writing faculty of Vermont College of Fine Arts for over 20 years.

Corinne Davis lives in Montpelier. She's the granddaughter of the late Deane C. Davis, Vermont's 74th governor and Corinne Eastman Davis (1901-51). Corinne is in the process of writing the last chapter of her grandmother's unfinished manuscript, titled *Love Song*, to be published in the near future.

Ann B. Day has been a member of PSOV since 1957. In the early days, the PSOV met in The Tavern in Montpelier. She is now ninety-five years old.

Robin Dellabough is a poet and editor. Her collection, *Double Helix* (2022), includes a Pushcart Prize-nominated poem; she is working on a second collection. Recent poems have appeared in *Gyroscope*, *Nixes Mate Review*, *Yellow Arrow*, *Stoneboat*, *Mom Egg Review*, *Blue Unicorn*, *Negative Capability*, and several anthologies. She recently relocated from a New York village to a Vermont village.

Harmony Belle Devoe (age sixteen), the Inaugural Vermont Youth Poet Laureate and a Northeast Regional Youth Poet Laureate runner-up, places a high value on the transformative power of words to educate, inspire, and create social impact. When not writing, she enjoys trail-running, baking, painting, theatre, snowboarding, and teatime. Harmony is the intern for the 2025 issue of *The Mountain Troubadour*.

Matthew Dickerson's poems have appeared in *Deep Wild*, *The Mountain Troubadour*, *Forgotten Ground Regained*, and *Tiny Seed* as well as the anthologies *Speculative Poetry* and *The Alliterative Revival* and the forthcoming *Cape Cod to Nova Scotia: Art, Ecology, Poetry of the Gulf of Maine*.

Trish Dougherty moved to Vermont in 1995 and has been working at Middlebury College ever since. She is an editor at *Zig Zag Lit Mag*, a local Addison County literary magazine. A graduate of the Bread Loaf School of English, she is also the author of *Forty Poems for Forty Pounds* (Cedar Lane Press).

Maggie Eaton, eldest of 12, grew up with poetry. In college, she participated in the University of Pittsburgh's International Poetry Forum and studied at the Yeats International Summer School in Sligo, Ireland. As a long-time Vermont educator, she continued to enjoy reading and writing poetry with students for many decades.

Julia H. Fonte is a retired psychiatric and hospice nurse living with her husband on old Vermont farmland. One of her poems was a finalist in the 2025 Vermont Writer's Prize. Her work appears or is forthcoming in *Touchstone*, *Steam Ticket*, *Northern New England Review*, *The Braided Way*, and *Verse-Virtual*.

Alice Wolf Gilborn founded the literary magazine, *Blueline*. She co-edited two collections of poetry *(Birchsong: Poetry Centered in Vermont)*, and authored a non-fiction book, *What Do You Do with a Kinkajou?* (Lippincott), an award-winning essay collection, *Out of the Blue* (Potsdam College Press), and two books of poetry, most recently, *Apples & Stones* from Kelsay Books.

Nancy Gordon has taught high school and college English in New Jersey and New Zealand, practiced law in the US, has been a reader all her life, and has been happy in recent years to be writing poems as well as reading them.

Cindy Ellen Hill is the author of *Wild Earth and Other Sonnets* (Antrim Press, 2021), *Elegy for the Trees* (Kelsay Books, 2022), and *Mosaic* (Wild Dog Press, 2024). Her full-length collection *Love in a Time of Climate Change* is forthcoming in 2025 from Finishing Line Press. Her essays on sonnets have appeared in *American Poetry Review* and *Unlikely Stories*. She twice won the Vermont Writer's Prize.

Whit Humphreys lives and writes poetry in Benson, Vermont.

Judith Janoo has published poems in journals and in two collections of poetry, *Just This* and *After Effects*. She is a contributing editor of the *Mountain Troubadour*. She lives in Vermont's Northeast Kingdom.

Anna N. Jennings writes poetry and creates handbound journals at her home studio in rural southern Vermont. At age fifty, Jennings returned to graduate school for a master's degree in art therapy followed by a creative writing certificate. She leads a weekly poetry group at a state correctional facility.

CurtB Johnson is a poet, author, and photographer living in Calais, Vermont. He was inspired during 2024's Poetry Month to begin writing poetry and sharing it at open mics in Central Vermont.

Joy hosts poetry events under the name rabbit&wolf throughout Central Vermont and is currently president of the Poetry Society of Vermont. Her poems are deeply personal, raw, and often erotic tiny memoirs within reimaginations of traditional forms. She intermittently posts then deletes first drafts on Instagram.

Kristine Korman has lived in the Mad River Valley of Vermont for ten years. Poetry resonates with her spirit. She consumes and composes it and has throughout her life. She majored in English at the City College of New York. She participates in writing groups. She is inspired by her family and the beautiful world around her.

Gordon Korstange lives in Saxtons River, Vermont, where he writes poetry and plays and performs Indian music on the bamboo flute.

George Longenecker lives in Pennsylvania with his wife and muse, Cynthia Martin, and their dog Aiko. His book *Star Route* was published by Main Street Rag. He looks for poetry in the paradoxical ways humans repeat their mistakes and reflect nature in their art.

Elizabeth McCarthy lives in an old farmhouse in the Northeast Kingdom of Vermont with her husband and cat. Retired from teaching, she began writing poetry during the pandemic, publishing four collections of poetry.

Her most recent chapbooks are: *Hard Feelings* (Finishing Line Press, 2024) and *Wild Silence* (Kelsay Books, 2024).

A longtime member of the PSOV, **Carol Milkuhn** is grateful to the PSOV for nurturing her interest in creative writing. In addition to being published in *The Troubadour* and other literary journals, she is the author of two poetry chapbooks, *In the Company of Queens* and *Modern Tapestries, Medieval Looms*.

David Mook has an MFA from Vermont College and teaches at Vermont State University Castleton. He won the 2024 Weybridge Haiku Contest. Recent publications include *Fatal Force: Poetic Justice, and Remembering Frost*, anthologies from Moonstone Press. David sponsors The Sarah Mook Poetry Contest for students in grades K-12. Learn more at www.sarahmookpoetrycontest.com.

Karen Morris is a poet and psychoanalyst in private practice in Montpelier. She is an Ambassador of Hope for Shared Hope International in their mission to eradicate sex trafficking of children. She is a transmitted teacher in the Soto Zen Buddhist tradition and a cofounder of Barre Zen Circle.

Erika Nichols-Frazer (she/her), editor of *The Mountain Troubadour*, is the author of *Staring Too Closely* (Main Street Rag, 2023) and *Feed Me: A Story of Food, Love and Mental Illness* (Casper Press, 2022). She holds an MFA from the Bennington Writing Seminars and has been nominated for a Pushcart Prize.

Scudder H. Parker's new volume of poetry and prose, *The Poem of the World*, will be published by Kelsay Books late winter of 2025. He lives with his wife Susan in Middlesex where he writes, gardens, and enjoys family friends and neighbors. Follow his new Substack at www.thesuddenthingitrustpoetry.substack.com.

Elaine Pentaleri served on the Burlington Writers Workshop board as editor of *Cold Lake Anthology* and *Mud Season Review*. She initiated The Green Mountain Book Festival. Her work appears in small presses and online publications. A book of poetry, *Dreamscape with Absinthe*, is forthcoming by Finishing Line Press.

Jennie Pollard has lived in Illinois, Arizona, Hawai'i, California, Colorado, Oklahoma, Texas, and now lives in Vermont. She graduated from The University of Hawai'i. Her poems have been published in anthologies, newspapers, and newsletters. Jennie reads locally, has been honored with several awards, and shares poems with family and friends.

Susan M. Sanders was born and raised in Vermont. She is a former single mother who earned two degrees with honors. Her poems have appeared in several journals and e-zines over the past thirty years and she was nominated for a Pushcart Prize in poetry in 2021.

Tom Schmidt, a retired humanities professor, is the author of thirteen books and four collections of poetry, most recently *Rowing with Either Oar* (Solum Literary Press, 2024) and *Stranger in Parodies* (Kelsay Books, 2025).

Ivy Schweitzer's poems appeared most recently in The New England Poetry Club's *Prize Winners' Anthology for 2024*. Her first collection, co-written with Al Salehi, is *Within Flesh: In Conversation with Our Selves and Emily Dickinson* (2024). Her debut solo collection, *Dividing Rivers*, will appear in 2025 from Finishing Line Press.

A social justice- & eco-activist with a background in the arts, literature, & environmental policy, **Ashley Anne Strobridge** (cover artist) is an Artist, Poet, Photographer, Writer, & Performer whose work is whimsical & impactful Nature photography, poetry, & paintings with literature, justice, ecology, and history tie-ins, available in cards, prints, books, & more.

Tamsen Turner is originally from Marshfield, Vermont and now resides in Albany, Vermont. She is a writer, singer, gamer, nonprofit finance professional, and sheep stepmom, among other things.

Kate Viens is a historian and editor by training who has spent her career working in New England museums. Raised in the salt air among the scrub oaks of southeastern Massachusetts, she writes poetry to explore our deep attachments to place and the moments in which it shapes our lives.

CD Williams currently lives in North Williston where he celebrates family, former students, and his Quaker community after spending forty years in Barre teaching school and working to help former residents of Brandon Training School adjust to life outside of institutions. Poetry is the music of his soul.

Rebecca Willis is a new poet inspired by her writing group in the Mad River Valley. She is enjoying the process of finding her poet's eye, incorporating her life in nature along with her background in astrophysics and interest in social justice in her work.

Jess Woolford's poetry appears in *Young Ravens Literary Review*, the museum of americana, *Book of Matches*, *Text Power Telling Magazine*, *The Ecological Citizen*, *Prairie Fire*, *CV2*, *The Winnipeg Free Press* and elsewhere. Raised in Vermont, Woolford now lives and writes on Treaty 1 Territory in Winnipeg, Manitoba.

David Kent Young, a Navy Veteran, is a resident of Stratton, Vermont, where he serves as Town Clerk and wrote its Town History. Kent has since self-published two children's books with his daughter and enjoys writing poetry to accompany his wife's photography—a hobby that has produced three self-published books.

FRIENDS OF PSOV

Please help support our many activities by becoming a Friend of PSOV or by honoring a PSOV member. To contribute, please make your donation online at poetrysocietyofvermont.org, under the Membership tab then Make a Donation.

PSOV is grateful for the generosity of the following individuals for their continued support:

Juliana Collins Anderson
Kathy Bonnez
Mary Cheyne
Alice Christian
Corinne Davis
Ann B. Day
Nancy Gilbert
Alice Gilborn
William Graham
Green Mountain Book Festival
Cindy Ellen Hill

Whit Humphreys
Kristine Korman
Elizabeth McCarthy
Kathleen McKinley
Joanne Mellin
Carol Milkuhn
Diane Swan
Geza Tatrallyay
Roger Watters
Carl Williams

ABOUT THE POETRY SOCIETY OF VERMONT

The Poetry Society of Vermont, founded in 1947, is a community of poets and friends of poetry who join in promoting enthusiasm for poetry through workshops, readings, and contests. Members have the opportunity to connect with other appreciative readers and writers of poetry and to publish in *The Mountain Troubadour*, PSOV's annual literary journal.

PSOV is committed to a value system of acceptance and inclusion. Our governance leads by example in creating and supporting a world that invites everyone to contribute to a culture of understanding across all communities. Everyone deserves access to the power of poetry and equitable resources, especially traditionally underrepresented and underserved populations. PSOV does not tolerate discrimination on the basis of race, gender, sexual orientation, religion, age, ability, or national origin.

MEMBERSHIP includes a copy of the journal, published annually. We welcome high school and college students, as well as appreciative writers and readers. To join, contact PSOV Membership Chair Jenn Brown at membership@poetrysocietyofvermont.org. Membership dues are tiered. To enroll online, visit the PSOV website at poetrysocietyofvermont.org (preferred) or mail your request to P.O. Box 914, Montpelier, VT 05601-0914. Please include your name, mailing address, telephone number, and email address. Additional copies of *Troubadour* may also be purchased through the website.

THE MOUNTAIN TROUBADOUR SUBMISSION GUIDELINES
SUBMISSION requires membership. Poems are accepted from December 15 to January 31. For complete guidelines, please visit the PSOV website.

CONTESTS AND AWARDS

TROUBADOUR AWARDS
Each year PSOV presents two awards to members, the Corinne Eastman Davis and Arthur Wallace Peach memorial awards, for poems published in the previous issue of the *Troubadour*. All member poems are eligible. Winners are announced in the spring, with an honorable mention for each. Winning poems are awarded a $20 prize.

CONTESTS

Each summer PSOV offers seven contests. The prize for winning poems is $50 and publication in the *Troubadour* the following year. The Carol and Arnold Abelson Award awards $25 to a second-place winner. Honorable mentions will be published with the winners in each of the seven contests. For complete guidelines, please visit the PSOV website.

CAROL AND ARNOLD ABELSON AWARD
An event or place that fosters opposition, controversy and/or social change. The event can be historical or reflect a current political situation, 40-line limit.

MARY MARGARET AUDETTE MEMORIAL AWARD
Light or humorous verse, 32-line limit.

J. RICHARD BARRY MEMORIAL AWARD
Vermont or country theme, 32-line limit

MARIAN GLEASON MEMORIAL AWARD
Any theme, 20-line limit.

GOLDSTEIN MEMORIAL AWARD
Any theme, 40-line limit.

LAURA J. SPOONER MEMORIAL AWARD
Best love poem, 40-line limit.

CHRIS WHITE MEMORIAL AWARD
Science, science fiction, or math theme, 25-line limit.

PSOV EXECUTIVE COUNCIL

The PSOV Executive Council is here to serve membership. If you would like to be in touch, please contact us at info@poetrysocietyofvermont.org.

President	Robyn Joy
Vice President/Recording Secretary	Maggie Eaton
Executive Secretary	David Hartnett
Treasurer	Buffy Aakaash
Membership Chair	Jennifer Brown
Web Manager/Workspace Administrator	Elizabeth McCarthy
The Mountain Troubadour Editor	Erika Nichols-Frazer
Contests Co-Chair	Juliana Anderson
Contests Co-Chair	Kristine Korman

www.ingramcontent.com/pod-product-compliance
Lightning Source LLC
Chambersburg PA
CBHW070121080526
44586CB00013B/1348